VOICES NEVER HEARD!!

MARYLYN BUTTAFUOCO AGUILAR

VOICES NEVER HEARD!!

DEDICATION

I dedicate this tale of my life in the "war zone" of inner cities in the 1960's to all of us who survived AND to those who lost their lives. Many have been able to move past the hatred and bigotry. We and the memories of those who died are a family.

VOICES NEVER HEARD!!

CONTENTS

VOICES NEVER HEARD!!

ACKNOWLEDGMENTS

I want to thank my son who urged me to follow my dream of an education and helped me to find my path. I am so grateful. I also thank my husband who supported me in my route as a trauma survivor. It has proven an amazing journey.

Preface

My story is one of an Italian American born in Brooklyn, moving to
Queens and then back to Brooklyn. I
grew up in a time in our history when the black cloud of hatred settled over
neighborhoods. Ghetto-like
life swallowed communities as racism burned the landscape. Shuddering
fear became the backdrop.
I could be education's poster child for the kid left behind. My husband has
recognized the trauma that
has painted my life. As a child everything felt like it was done to me. I
reacted always with survival in
mind.
We need to force the conversation about race – with all its faces. Becky
who helped me edit tells me
this sign is for me – real women don't have hot flashes, they have power
surges.
My memories of those years and my pain remain clear and still I have
gradually grown and changed.

VOICES NEVER HEARD!!

CHAPTER ONE

FIRST EXPERIENCE WITH BIGOTRY

"THERE IS NOTHING MORE FRIGHTFUL THAN IGNORANCE IN ACTION."
-JOHANN WOLFGANG VON GOETHE

I saw so much bigotry as child that I was traumatized. Complete and stubborn intolerance and reason-less judgment is a frightening state of being. The very first experience of prejudice that I can remember was when I was about 8 years old. My family moved to Queens, New York when I was 4
years-old. The new neighborhood on 208th street in Hollis Queens, New York seemed nice but I really loved Brooklyn. We had everyone there - all my cousins, aunts and uncles, grandma and grandpa. This was our new home. I went to Catholic school, St. Pascal Baylon, from first to fourth grade. Nuns were stern with strict rules of discipline to be followed. As students, we complied with their direction and submitted to authority. With my parents' marriage difficulties, money became an issue and I had to switch schools to attend the local public school, P.S. 134 in Queens. In the midst of this change, the 60's and Civil rights movements were rampant . I saw the neighborhood begin to transform.

My parents spoke Italian as their first language and I used English with friends. Italians were very strict about speaking another language in front of anyone who didn't speak a foreign language. So we all had to speak English. As a child I loved playing double Dutch, a city rope skipping game where two ropes are twirled like an eggbeater with a third child jumping within. I was very good at it. The community was entering a new phase which saw most Caucasian people moving... **we stayed**. In one of my memories I was playing jump rope and I was so happy. I then wanted to play double dutch so I went to the local hardware store and got my very own rope. We kids did not like the cord strand; we liked the wire rope. I asked if anyone wanted to play double dutch with me and soon had the necessary friends to play. When finished, two teenage black girls about 16 years-old came up to us and bullied only me. They pushed me and screamed in my face, telling me to give them my rope. Having already rolled my rope, I said no. Their response was to assure me that they would "beat my ass!" My heart raced, at eight- years old I was so scared. I gave them my rope and thought to myself, "why didn't they take the other girl's rope? Why only mine?"

My frustration boiled over and I cried at my helplessness. When I could calm myself a little, I asked the other girl who was a year younger than I was why the two girls had only taken my rope and not hers. "Why didn't they push and scream at you?" She said, because you're white!!! "I thought white?? I am a sheet on a bed or color of a crayon?? I didn't understand what she meant. I went in the house crying, asking my father, "am I white??" He said, what are you talking about? Where did you get that idea?" I told him about the rope and that these girls stole mine because I was white. What a lesson. I was not taught bigotry in my home. I learned it from this neighborhood and the streets. Suddenly at a very young age, my eyes were completely opened. I attended my new school where I was the only white Italian American child in my class. I looked around and even at 10, I knew I was going to be the target of abuse.

Everyday the kids would call me names like white patty, white cracker or whitey. I began feeling so uncertain and started getting a complex. The other children – both boys and girls - would stare at me and ridicule me constantly. When papers were passed in class, they would say, "give it to whitey." The teacher had no control over what was happening. Teachers all held fear for their lives as well. I once heard a student say that if this teacher bothers me, my mamma will come down here and wop his ass.

I thought to myself that maybe my mother was afraid to do that to the teacher. But as I grew older, I realized that violence was not the way to handle things. The kids at school in that time period told me that every Friday was "feel" day. I didn't know what that meant and thought the word used was really to be "field" day. I came from catholic school. My interpretation of field day was totally different from anything I could have expected. Each Friday, boys and girls would feel each other up. I would so hate walking the halls on Fridays alone. I had no idea what they were attempting to do. "Boy!!" did I soon realize what this gauntlet meant. If I had to do anything on a Friday, I would run as fast I could to avoid being caught in the halls alone. As most school kids looked forward to Friday, I did not!

Chapter Two
THE VIOLENCE ESCALATES

"ASK A MAN WHAT HIS GREATEST FEAR IS ABOUT SERVING JAIL TIME, AND HE WILL ALMOST INEVITABLY SAY HE FEARS BEING RAPED. WHAT CAN WE DEDUCE FROM THE FACT THAT JAIL IS TO MEN WHAT LIFE IS TO SO MANY WOMEN?" —SORAYA CHEMALY

It was a very cold winter day and at times the school staff would let the children into the gym after lunch because it was so frigid outside. I would never eat in school, I would go home for lunch. On occasion if I had lunch money I would get White Castle hamburgers or pizza. There were not many fast foods back then. I used to try to return to school later so I did not have much contact with the other kids but this one day I finished my pizza and it was still early. I really did not want to go into the building but it was so cold and I didn't have the right clothing, just a coat with no gloves or hat. No one was in the gym and I was happily relieved. All of a sudden five boys jumped out and ran toward me-four blacks and one Puerto Rican. I saw them and ran but they were too fast. They caught me and threw me to the gymnasium floor. Just a week before my father bought me some beautiful earrings in Chinatown, New York City. These were a beautiful jade and gold - hearts with a jade carved into the shape of a heart. My foreboding rose and I didn't know what they were trying to do but I knew it was not good. The boys were holding down my hands mostly to get my arms down. The others were spreading my legs apart and then Puerto Rican guy got on top of me. All I could think was "what is going on?" "what's going on?"

I twisted and turned and somehow got away. This was utterly horrifying. I lost one of my jade earrings but I still had my dignity. I never found my other earring. I was just too scared to go back there. I naively thought someone might return it to the lost and found or even the custodian might find it. However, no one did. I told my dad that I lost the earring but not my experience and how I lost it. Something so special given to me by my dad became a memory of depravity and immorality. Another similar incident took place when I had to use the girls' bathroom. As I left the stall to wash my hands, five blacks girls said "oh, wow, a white girl." "Let's see what she looks like." I thought to myself in the sixth grade, "what do they mean, what does she look like?" They began working to take my clothes off! They violently shoved me into the corner of the bathroom and I remember banging into the large radiator. They were attempting to pull my underwear off! There was one large girl pinning my arms and holding me in a locked position. Wrestling me under my arms, she dragged me into that corner while the others laughed, fighting me to jerk my legs up so that I was lifted about two feet off the bathroom floor. One girl was pulling my underwear off. As I battled for my freedom, I remember looking up at the ceiling and seeing toilet paper stuck and wadded into balls.

I was trying desperately to stay focused to wrench out of this situation but it seemed hopeless. I felt trapped, terrified, and so very vulnerable. I knew I had this same trial with the five boys. I did not think I was going to get away. My head was spinning and my thoughts raced as I replayed the flashback to that day in the gym. I felt my stomach churn because I realized that my teacher wouldn't wonder where I was nor would he even care. I kept fighting and kicking my legs as the girl ripped my underwear down to my hip. I continued to kick and struggle and they dropped my legs. The very big girl finally let go, too. I scurried from that restroom so fast-all the while pulling my underwear up with one hand.

I was so afraid. Being extremely skinny I twisted my way out of that one, too. I dashed back to my class on the top floor, completely out of breath. The teacher noted my startled face and that I was panting from my sprint away from an ordeal but he asked no questions. Even though I was extremely late for class, he did not care. I could have been killed and yet he showed no sign of distress. From that point I always wore shorts under my skirts; I purposely went to the first floor bathroom thinking it had fewer students but, I was mistaken. I tried to hold my urine. What an impossible situation. When I simply had to use the restroom I made sure I could get to the sink closest to the door to wash my hands. I needed to escape if necessary. Fear was forever my companion. I felt the school officials were not burdened by what happened or my safety. As a child that was painful to discover because I had always believed that adults would try to protect children.

I was fortunate to leave five minutes before the dismissal bell rang. Exiting the building those few minutes early provided something of a safety net. Fights inevitably broke out when the school was dismissed. It seemed to me the kids loved the chaos and I could avoid most of it. We had special permission to leave early. It felt like I was in a war zone and I made sure I raced down those stairs to my brother's and sister's classrooms. My heart pounded as I waited for them to get ready to go home. I needed to beat that bell before it rang. This nightmare was hair-raising. I had only five minutes to go to each of their classrooms for first and second graders. They were young and pokey. My panic and sense of urgency made me determined and persistent. The school was like an oppressive prison with a large monster lurking out of view, ready to destroy you. As a child feeling this way, I told my mom that I had a stomach ache every day, hoping not to return. That didn't work. I had to go to school.

This was elementary school. Can you imagine? With all the fear and survival tactics I had no education beyond fourth grade. So much violence! We just didn't learn anything. None of the students seemed to want an education. There were probably four white students in the entire building and I was the single white girl in my class. Talk about segregation; I lived it! Violence and cruelty in every shape and form were everywhere. Stealing was prevalent, rape always possible, and any other type of aggressive, forceful behavior were school hallmarks. Guns and knives were found in the Junior High and the High Schools. Let's not forget drugs. Heroin was a prominent drug of choice then. Hate, fear, and racism of the most startling degree surrounded me.

I was a very nervous and apprehensive child. This environment was like a deranged zoo where many times the kids would walk on desks, dump trash on the floor, throw papers everywhere, and hang out the windows screaming. The classes had metal bars on the windows... now I understand why. I never knew anything like this with 6th grade cursing and threatening teachers. When kids would yell at a teacher, the rest of the class would join and laugh. I was so overwhelmed in watching this upside down world where my training as a child was in such opposition. One day we had a substitute teacher who was a black woman and the kids said let's be nice to her because she is black. I thought to myself how much I hated this school. There was, of course, a different set of rules for blacks.

I was taught to respect any adult. One of the awful mantras I learned right away was, "you put us in slavery." I spoke to my parents and told them we put blacks in slavery. My parents responded that our ancestors came from Italy and wanted to know what I was talking about. I said that they kept telling me this at school and on the streets. I was no longer a good and respectable pupil. My peers had won. My persona was now tough and bitter. I was changing and I knew it. I didn't like that but there seemed to be no choice for survival.

My regular teacher was Italian but I had no respect for him in allowing this behavior. As I look back over time, I recognize that he was also a captive of this place and time. This was his livelihood. They would terrorize him and tell their parents that the white teacher was picking on them. All he really wanted to do was to teach the class. The parents would come in and tell their kids, "I will beat his ass, don't worry." We were all hostages in this violent, lawless place. It was frightening to watch parents coming into the class. They would scream savagely and the sound would send chills through my body. I could feel the instinctual fear and I would get a visceral response. I remember the teacher across the hall from my classroom. Stress was too much and he had a heart attack and died. He spent most of his time trying to discipline the students as well as instruct. I would hear him across the hall constantly repeating a list of don't s: "don't run out the door, don't jump around, don't throw trash". Always trying to control his class, he would be called *old man whitey* as they made fun of his gray hair and skin color. It seemed to me that he inherited the worst of the students. In New York City schools, administrators would corral the most unfavorable students in a classroom with others like them. My class was not a pretty picture either. When he died, the kids showed no deference and talked about him being just an old white man anyway. I thought to myself how sad it was to think that he could be someone's grandpa.

Growing up in this neighborhood was appalling. Bigotry was everywhere. There was a big black girl who lived on my block who utterly hated me. She was so big. I was only 60 pounds and she always wanted to beat me up, telling me so. I would stand up to her and the kids would gather like the crowds in the Roman Colosseum, watching me get man-handled. My knees would be scraped and burned from the cement. She would grab a handful of my hair and drag me on the concrete like I was a rag doll. I was so tired of being laughed at, abused, and mistreated. All because I am white. Anger spewed from my small body. The girl who once was me was changing.

Today there is talk about bullying. I have seen it all. I had a good friend who was regularly going through the same thing. She suffered from discrimination, abuse, and violent attacks. She, too, was white. My friend lived off Francis Lewis Blvd and had her own terror to face. When I would visit her on a weekend, I had to pass 207th Street get to her house. That was probably the most frightening block of all. This street had a very bad reputation. No one wanted to fight or debate with anyone from 207th Street. I would run like hell. It was as if you had to enter a dark room with no lights and try to find the 9 door. Like a scary movie, you never knew what would happen. I would be so glad I made it to my friend's house without being beaten or verbally attacked. My friend and her family suffered in this strange world just like mine.

My older brother attended the school across from mine, Linden Junior High 192. He went through his personal Hell, too. I looked up to my oldest brother and asked what happened to him at school. The initiation button to start a fight was, "hey, white boy, you killed my brothers?" My brother told me that they kept staring at him to start a fight and say, "what you looking at white boy?" It was like my experience. The story seemed always the same but with different characters. I remember a time, saving money from cashing in bottles at Ruth and Ruby's candy store on Hollis Avenue. I asked one of my friends to go with me to Jamaica Avenue which was a big shopping area. I wanted the new Barbie doll that came out because it twisted and turned. Exiting the Q2 Queens bus on Hollis Avenue, two big black girls carrying knives approached and one put a knife to my throat, demanding money. I didn't have any more money because I spent it on the bus fare and the doll. I can still remember the feel of the point of the blade at my throat. They made me open the bag only to see my Barbie doll which I hoped they wouldn't take. It took me a long time to save for that doll. They also made us empty our pockets. For some reason they let us go and we ran like lightning!!

Who can forget poor Elizabeth, the blind woman, who lived on 208 th and ll2 th Avenue down the block from me? Elizabeth was an angel to me in this dark and evil environment. She was tall, very neatly dressed, very slender and always stood straight. She was an older woman who lived with her mother and father. I remember to this day her wearing such beautiful Irish or Scottish patterns. Whenever she would walk up the block, we would go with her to the grocery store and back home. Not that we were protection, but I loved Elizabeth. I thought of her often and wondered about her life. She would bring back the kindness that I was losing and awareness the innocence torn from me. I would hold her hand. I remember how long, soft, and warm it was. Elizabeth would ask us about our day. With a white and red cane in one hand, I would hold her other hand. I would see her move the cane back and forth to make sure nothing was in her way. I thought that she seemed so happy. If she only knew what people in her neighborhood who could see were doing. Even as a child, I wondered how Elizabeth was so happy living in darkness without sight. Although I had decent eye sight, I was in my own kind of darkness because of these horrible events. The people possessing good sight were so miserable. I couldn't understand it. I couldn't weigh and balance the factors. Eyesight is such a wonderful gift. How is it that so much hate overshadows the gift of sight? My friend and I would wait for Elizabeth in front of Associated Grocery until her baggage wheel-cart was filled with her needs. Stopping at her home, her mother would give us some candy. After a while we knew candy was coming.

One day, I was walking through the halls in school and I saw what looked like a big clump of blood with lumps in it. I didn't know what it was so, I told my friend to look at it. We couldn't figure it out. It looked like jelly but it was very dark red. I heard later that some boys raped a girl. At that point in elementary school, I knew what rape was. Can you believe that? It reminded me of the day they tried to rape me but I escaped. That could have been me, I told myself. Going to gym I told the teacher, "look" and all she said was to walk over the clumps of blood. I remember it clearly being right outside the gym door in the hall. The trauma and shock still live within me. All that I learned as a child was topsy-turvy. My emotions consisted only of fear, anxiety, and horror. I never felt safe! The teachers and faculty seemed 10 to ignore all the havoc and turmoil. They were desensitized and school was a place where dread lurked in every hall and around every corner. There was no protection and no safety net.

Where do you go for help when your pleas are ignored? The cries landed on deaf ears. The school staff was so afraid of racial ramifications and lived in trepidation. Life in this war-torn arena could be easily sacrificed. The school across the street had students who threw teachers out the second floor windows. Teachers feared the students and the parents. Students had raped one teacher I knew, leaving her face scarred by the knife-wielding one. I knew her personally. I met her as an adult and we shared our experiences of the horrors then. She taught in Brooklyn. Let us say she tried to teach only to be treated as some disposable lump of flesh.

Chapter Three
My Education Affected

"Poverty is the worst form of violence."
—Mahatma Gandhi

We were all threatened and panic-stricken. I asked my parents repeatedly if we put the blacks into slavery because I needed reassurance after constantly being told this. I remember another incident in class when a new student came. He needed a pencil and asked the girl next to him if she had one. She told him to ask the white girl because they always had pens, papers, and pencils. Was I doing something wrong to be prepared? Another time a girl grabbed my pencil in recess, threw it on the floor, and told me to pick it up. She ordered,"white girl, pick up my pencil!" The whole class laughed. I did not want to pick it up but I did. "Now you are a slave." They all laughed. I was the butt of the joke and I felt very small and alone. I thought to myself I am Italian. I realized that ethnicity was not the issue but my skin color was. I was painted with the same brush the white brush. I knew it was getting to the point where I had to learn how to fight even though my parents told me ignore them.

How do you ignore throngs of angry kids? This was every day. I couldn't think straight with my dignity shredded just like my chance for education. There was no civilization. I was being carved into something that they pictured. I stopped bringing pencils, paper, and pens. I thought that would do it. Nothing solved this problem. Knowing my father had been a professional boxer, I pleaded, "please!! Teach me how to box, won't you? He said, "no, you are a girl and Italian one. It is not right to fight!" One day I came home with scratches all over my face. My father was so angry. I told him they called me whitey again and the girl starting swinging and scratched my face, leaving long open scrapes. This was entertainment to everyone and they laughed uproariously. I can still remember feeling the stinging on my face as I tell this story. When I would wash my face, it would burn. My face looked as if I had been attacked by a large cat. I was fortunate that my eyes were OK. I looked at my face in the mirror like this for days. I did not know what was worse being attacked or wearing that face for weeks. It seemed to take forever to heal. I wondered if my face now would be scarred now for life. I was tired of others asking the question what happened to your face. I still wear some scars on my face where I was attacked. They are light but still present... While she was hitting me in the face, the others were hitting me from behind. Those scars, too, are still here-they are internal. I had to find a way to get some kind of control over this for it to stop! I just knew I was a target. My skin color was an object and symbol of their hatred. I had light colored hair, green eyes, and ringlets. My hair was always a focus for being yanked and tugged. So, I would always tie it back. I wore shorts under my skirts. Both boys and girls were always trying to look up your skirt. It never occurred to me to do this to another.

Life was a test of endurance. I really couldn't grasp the excitement of looking under someone's skirt. There was a sense of making the other person less somehow. Shorts became my life saver and hair tied back was easier than having it pulled or having gum slapped into it. They liked putting gum in white people's hair because that would need to be cut and get all tangled. I brought no more paper, notebooks or pens to school. So I sat in class just to wait for lunch and a little before 3pm because I could leave earlier. I remember always looking toward the classroom window wondering what it would be like to be in a different school. The memory of my earlier school was all I had. There I had found total discipline, students who did homework, and where we all learned. I wondered what they were learning 12 now and what I was missing. I always sat in the back corner by myself to pull myself from unwanted contention and jealousy. I discovered that I should wear the same clothing to prevent being made fun of or having them ripped if they were new. Jealousy was a common factor. There are jokes about not having anything nice, but this was tribal law. You were not supposed to have anything new. At the school across the street, white guys were forced to give up their leather jackets and walk home with nothing. You needed to learn these rules of this strange community. The school across the street the kids were bringing scissors to school. They were cutting white guys hair. In that time period the style was long hair for guys. One incident they tried to cut one guys hair and cut his neck.

Chapter Four
My 6 Year-old Brother Beaten

"If by my life or death I can protect you, I will." - J. R. R. Tolkien

I was in class one day when a friend of mine asked the teacher if she could speak to me. The teacher wouldn't allow that but I could see the fear pulsing from my friend's face. I ran to her. She told me there was blood covering the steps and my brother had been beaten and was bleeding. The stairs in this school were concrete and metal. I couldn't imagine my little brother falling down them. He had been pushed and beaten at the bottom. I saw the blood. I was terrified. She told me the whole cafeteria was clapping while watching him being thrashed. My unfortunate little brother had such poor eyesight and his glasses were so thick that without them he was almost blind. My friend told me to check the nurse's office, but he wasn't there. Where could he be? I went to his class and the teacher thought he might be in the principal's office. Yes, there he was, holding his bloody nose. I told the principal he was my brother and she responded that she was calling your mom now.

I asked him what happened. "Where are your glasses?" The glasses were broken, totally shattered. I heard the principal lie to my mother on the phone. She said he fell down the stairs breaking his glasses which hit his nose and eyes. I grabbed the phone from her and told mom the truth. The barbaric students threw him down the stairs. The principal was afraid to tell the truth and this little boy of seven could have been horribly injured. My brother could have died overnight from head trauma . She feared a race riot would break out and for her own life. Elementary school! I refused to leave him and waited for my mother to arrive. He really needed help now because he couldn't see without his glasses. Luckily his nose was not broken and only the bridge of his nose cut. While waiting he told me the story. He had finished lunch and wanted to make a paper plane; he had just learned. This was quite the achievement with his very poor eyesight. It seemed that the kids who hurt him couldn't bear to see him happily enjoying his accomplishment and shredded it, leaving it on the cafeteria floor. They chased him up the stairs, punching him until they could throw him down the stairs and stomp on him. I was furious and learned which boy had started the attack. I knew where his classroom was, skipped class, and waited until he needed to use the bathroom. He was alone and I grabbed him, hurling him fiercely against the wall. My dad had relented and taught me to box. I practiced with a vengeance, growing more skillful and powerful every day. I had decided to defend myself and now was the only girl who knew how to box.

One afternoon at recess as I sat by myself I watched a circle of girls seated around this one girl. This happened in the classroom. I was curious about what they had or what they were doing. One girl was giving instructions on how to masturbate and explained that she did it every night before sleep. The group seemed mesmerized. The girl had her skirt pulled up and her hands in her underwear. One girl leaned over to look at her hand in the underwear and pulled it forward. I was young and knew this was wrong. I couldn't believe it! I walked away. Doing this routine in the classroom so disgusting!! I never wanted ever take anything from that girl not even a paper that was passed in the classroom. My education by this time was nonexistent. I was only a placeholder avoiding being truant. My stomach ached as I wondered about this behavior for my little brother and sister. One day I decided to go visit my 14 little brother. I didn't see him and the teacher pointed to a group of giggling kids. They had him in the closet with his pants down. I screamed!! The teacher was reaction-less. These instructors were frozen objects, totally oblivious. Where was discipline and civilized behavior?

My older 16 year-old brother asked me to go with him to Jamaica Avenue one Saturday morning. He gave me money to buy records, 45's and told me he would wait outside while I paid. He never had a lot of patience and double parked in front of the Mays store. I picked out the records he wanted and waited in line as people cut in front of me because I was a little white girl. Without warning a big black man about 25 years-old pulled me to a corner and demanded my change. I refused and the security guard watching this simply declined to act. I kept looking at the security guard hoping he would intervene but he ignored my plight. The 25 year-old aggressor ordered me to jump up and down to see if I had more money in my pockets. He rejected my pleas to be released until I gave him my change. As busy as Jamaica Avenue was, I could still hear my brother beeping the car horn for me to hurry up. I could not go anywhere. My brother finally came in to see all of this and I told him the guy wanted his record money.

My brother wasn't the least bit afraid. He dealt with this every day in 192 Linden Junior High. "You bothering my little sister? **YOU** jump up and down! **Now!**" The fellow was so scared that he did and my brother took his change. Then my brother had extra money. What a cement jungle! You had to wear a suit of armor. Another time this same brother we were walking his girlfriend home from our place on 208th to 216th street. As we walked several black guys surrounded the three of us. They terrified his girlfriend and me. My brother directed the two of us to move to the side and he proceeded to take off his belt. He was ready to tackle that circle. They saw that this was no regular white guy and figured they were going to get more than that for which they had bargained. Rolling up his belt showed a huge buckle which would be a nasty weapon. They let us go. All this was a strange head game. These were terrible times. Frightening and corrosive to your spirit.

On the weekends, I would go visit my friend who lived on Francis Lewis Blvd. We had been planning on going shopping with her mom. It was hot and all the windows in the car were down. All of a sudden I heard a crash. Some kids threw a bottle in the window of the passenger side where my friend was sitting. I was right behind and although the glass shattered with it flying everywhere, we weren't hurt. The kids that threw the bottle screamed at my friend's mother, "get out of here white lady before we throw a jar at you!" We went back to her house. I vacuumed the glass out of her beautiful hair. I can distinctly remember the details. The jar was a Nescafe instant coffee container made of very heavy glass. As I vacuumed the car seat, I remembered the day my father and I took a cab during hot weather. The driver told us to roll up the windows because that was the area where bottles were routinely hurled. This was Brooklyn and it had happened in Queens. The city was a battlefield.

My mother began to see this for herself when she got her first job at White Castle. One day my mom was at work on the corner of Francis Lewis and Hollis Avenue. I overheard her talking about the two teenage guys who helped paint our house. They had come into the restaurant for hamburgers and she saw one get stabbed in the back while waiting in line. White Castle had counter service back then and both the guys jumped over the counters for safety. Mom's uniform was covered in blood. It was very hard to be calm. We thought our mother was stabbed. My mother reassured us that it wasn't her blood. She told us that she had held the one boy until the police and ambulance arrived. I was told that the black detective, who was first to come to the scene of the crime warned the thugs to run because more police where on there way. Where was justice? My Mother heard the black customers saying that white people were devils and that the hamburger shop should be called black castle. After the stabbing I never knew what happened to those boys.

A friend came to my house where many in the area played stick-ball and one of the girls up the block started a fight with her. The fight grew more intense and my friend was really pounding the girl. her mom came outside, picked my friend up, and ferociously slammed her to the ground. This woman was so large that she looked like a colossus. My friend was only about 11 years-old. She ran and left her baby brother with me. That poor girl was petrified. She had already been struck by glass in her car. Life seemed like a flow of one tortured experience following another.

Springtime was coming and I remember mom buying a few new dresses in Mays on Jamaica Avenue for me. One dress in particular was my favorite. It was white and pink gingham with a white lace collar with ruffles down the sleeves. I wanted to wear it to school so very much even though I knew something might damage it. Mom said I could but reminded me that it was for Easter. I took a chance and wore it to school. Before dismissal I went to get my little brother and sister. I had cut through the schoolyard. All at once a black girl stepped out, "she think she cute?" I was just trying to leave to go home. I wasn't looking for trouble. The black kids used to play a game called best man hit to start a fight. Because they had no reason to fight you; they chose a middle person to hit and that one then hit you. I hated this game. I was so worried about my brother and sister that I didn't want to fight, and I knew how to brawl now. Any minute the bell would ring and I screamed to my brother and sister, "just go home! You know the way! I will be OK." Instead of playing that detestable game, I pushed the middle girl out-of-the-way and punched the daylights out of the first girl who started the fight. The girl fell to the ground. I jumped on top of the girl . The bell rang and that was it. I was jumped I don't know how many kids were hitting me. The more I was hit on the top of my head the more I pounded her head on the school yard cement. The school aid told the officer I started the fight He responded with disbelief that I would do something to all these kids. I told the aid your scared just like every other school official. You're a liar? I was glad the police arrived quickly. It's probably what saved me. I was very disoriented and nervous.

Those kids crowded around the police car. The police drove me right to my house. It took several minutes to leave because they blocked the squad car and some were jumping on the car as if all sanity were gone. I remember seeing this on the news where cars were flipped and jumped on like an amusement ride. Even in a police car I feared the mob and destruction to the car. The officer assured me that I would be all right. The attacker had ripped my favorite dress. I was so unhappy. I wanted so much to wear that dress for Easter. Now, just like the neighborhood, it, too, was destroyed.

Those kids crowded around the police car. The police drove me right to my house. It took several minutes to leave because they blocked the squad car and some were jumping on the car as if all sanity were gone. I remember seeing this on the news where cars were flipped and jumped on like an amusement ride. Even in a police car I feared the mob and destruction to the car. The officer assured me that I would be all right. The attacker had ripped my favorite dress. I was so unhappy. I wanted so much to wear that dress for Easter. Now, just like the neighborhood, it, too, was destroyed.

Chapter Five
My crucial Years

"And the day came when the risk to remain tight in a bud was more painful than the risk it took to blossom." —Anais Nin

One day after playing double dutch, I sat on my stoop. Two girls walked by and my little brother said, "Mary, those girls are on my bus". One turned and said, "shut up you 'Fucken' four eyed fool." I asked, "who do you think you're talking to?" I had heard this statement constantly: "if you are talking about my family, you are talking about me." It was an open call to fight. I loved and would protect my little brother. She taunted, "what you going to do about it?" Girls like that would wear long chains with keys around their necks to intimidate you while they swung them. She took off the chain, "I am going to beat your ass!" I punched her so hard in the face she told her friend to help her. Her friend wanted no part of a girl boxer. I growled, "if **you** move, I'll be the one to beat **your ass!**" My older brother heard the screams and raced downstairs. He pulled us apart. I told him 207th street will come that's where she lived. Within twenty minutes the whole block was full of people. There were adults and children; all coming to beat me up, a sixth grader. They had sticks with nails in them screaming," get that while girl!" The mob was chanting repeatedly, "get that white girl!" Even to this day, I can hear that battle cry. The hatred was sickening. My mom tried to drive her car through the throng but couldn't make a way. She called the police and they scattered but the police had to circle the block all night to protect us. The police told my mom,"you better get her out of here or they'll kill her". My little brother told me he was afraid of that girl because she was a big mouth on his bus and a huge trouble maker. My little sister and brother were minorities on the bus. That is when I moved to Brooklyn.

I did not move back to Brooklyn officially after 7th grade. My mom had taken in a 17-year-old boy. He was a like a brother to me. He was walking

28

home from work on Hollis Avenue one day and two black guys asked him for a cigarette but he didn't have extra and wouldn't be paid for a few days. Quickly one whistled and a bunch of black guys stormed him and beat him badly and stole his watch, cigarettes, and suede jacket. They pummeled him, stepped on him with their feet breaking his rib which punctured his lung.

I will always remember him screaming and wailing in pain that night. The screaming and wailing from the agonizing pain he walked from 204th street to 208 th with a punctured lung. He had to walk four 17 blocks home, doubled in pain and no one helped. Banged on our front door and fell to the floor. I could barely contain my fear – so much blood. The detective came but never found his assailants. My older brother who loved this guy went crazy and ran out to Hollis Avenue, trying to find who did this. The police followed and made him get in the squad car. There would be no justice.

The next day I walked home from school heard a few black guys bragging about beating a white guy. I dropped my books, hoping to hear names. They laughed like it was some game. I saw the blood on the sidewalk. I was terribly afraid. You never knew what would happen next. We had to attend school but learning was never really an option. I remember the blacks saying they could not get an education. I thought, "what about me?: There was no way teachers could instruct.

I lost the school years 5,6,7, and 8 by the time I moved to Elmont in Nassau County. I was lost I and couldn't keep up with the work. I was like a fourth grader in junior high school and moving on to high school. It was awful. I wanted so much to learn but this atmosphere blocked me. I felt like I was so stupid. I only had a 4th grade education. News on television would report upheaval and racial demonstrations. What a scary world. The more the media reported, the greater the abuse in the schools. My older brother was in fights every day. The few of us had to stick together. No one today would be able to guess the horrors we endured.

One day the doorbell rang and the mother of a guy who had been fighting my brother stood there. She pulled a gun on my mom. She wanted to kill my brother who was in Brooklyn that day. The woman kept repeating, "I want your son!" My mom's friend called the police and she ran. Of course, she denied having a gun.

A German Shepherd bit my friend's little brother. They were popular dogs in that era. The man told the dog to go after the little white kid who was about seven or eight. It was enjoyment for him to watch the dog go for the child's jugular. The dog bit his neck and the little boy was smart enough to put his arms up. The dog mauled his wrists and neck while this man watched. Someone noticed and came to help. The owner called the dog off. I have held this in my whole life. Again, no justice came. The doctors in the little boy's hospital reported that he would have died if the attack had continued.

At the end of my sixth year, my teacher told me he was promoting me to 7th grade. I was shocked-we had learned nothing all year. I asked, "really, how?" Students were passed to keep State funding. I suffered all my life because of this mentality. I went through life with the loss of an education. I tried several times throughout my life to receive a high school diploma in adult education, but couldn't keep up without any baseline of study. The next year at Linden Junior High on Hollis avenue was even worse than the elementary school. My brother in the 9th grade would continue to Andrew Jackson High School.

I was a bit happy on my first day because there was another white girl in my class. I might not be the only target. She was a very pretty Italian girl and the kids always made fun of her. They beat her so badly that she was hospitalized. I was so worried for the girl. She recovered. She shared with me that her injuries might prevent her from having children. We in the minority protected each other. My brother's friend, who was a bit older than he, would pick me up before the bell would ring to walk me home safely. He died at a young age but I will never forgot him. I think of him every time I hear the Happenings' song, "I Got Rhythm." His girlfriend commuted to school on the city bus on Hollis Avenue. While waiting for the bus one afternoon, the kids who were so envious of her beautiful hair battered her so severely that she fell into a coma. They pounded her head on the pavement and stepped on her. The authorities never discovered the assailants. A year after being released from the hospital, she complained to my friend of a headache. She died in his arms. My friend was devastated what a horror the girl you love dying in your arms.

I feel in my heart that today's technology might have saved her. She was 16 and left her boyfriend shattered, living in an emotional prison of loss. He was 24 when he died. The media at this time continued their reports of torched houses, muggings, looting, and Molotov cocktails exploding through windows. The streets were scenes of savagery and cruelty. The hate campaign was overwhelming and widespread. All the great cities of Chicago, New York, Los Angeles, Detroit, and some in New Jersey were under attack. I had nightmares constantly. I dreamed a man came through my window at night to burn down the house. Many kids were making homemade guns called zip guns.
It was a turbulent time. You could even find razors in hair for protection. My older brother was constantly fighting. The school intercom blared once that all officials should immediately come to the class on the second floor that was my brother's class. Kids were tossing desks and the police were called. I remember sitting in class hearing the frenzied chanting,"we shall overcome! we shall overcome!" while they pounded their fists on the desks and stomped their feet. They were copying the militant protesters on television. It sounded like a stampede of horses blowing out your mind. I wanted to disappear. We were forever on guard for our next assault. There was physical violence and head games just to start a brawl. These kids would manufacture instances where you had wronged them. It was gas-lighting in the worst form.

The houses in Queens were close and one night I felt hot in my sleep and smelled smoke. I heard crackling and got up to see sparks. Flames engulfed the house across the street. We got out of our house waiting for the fireman to arrive. These men risked their lives for unnecessary destruction.

Fires were started to prove a point. As a child I just didn't' understand this. These local terrorists wanted power and control. I experienced night terrors, triggered continually by TV's coverage of screaming and angry Civil Rights protesters. All the civil rights leaders were constantly in the media. Their faces always had that hard stare only a victim of racism would understand. In fact they seemed to encourage angry action. The future held violence, too, over the attack on Rodney King in LA. I was so scared I remember these events like they were yesterday. Ironically it happened in April, the same month Martin Luther King was killed.

There were times I thought hiding under my bed that would protect me. One day when I was playing stick ball, a girl started a fight with me and I soundly beat her. I knew how to box then. She lied to her mother and told her that I started the fight. The mom came up the block to my house and I ran inside, locking the door. She beat the door with a belt. I could hear the belt buckle pounding on the door from mom's bedroom. "Come out here, whitey, I am going to beat you with this belt!" I had been defending myself. I hid under my mom's bed. These mixed messages came at me all the time – someone would attack me without reason and when I stood up for myself, I was again attacked.

In my heart I always knew it was a losing battle. It seemed to me that I was fighting with one hand tied behind my back. Hiding under that bed I was terrified. I imagined she would break down the door. The idea that this big black woman would reach me and pummel and whip me with the belt nonstop kept running through my head. She shrieked in rage but not one person on my block called the police. It seemed as if she would never stop. She finally left. There seemed no laws to protect us. Mom asked about the marks on our white door and I told her about this episode.

This was the summer before junior high, Linden Junior High, one of the worst schools in Queens. My elementary school was a developing ground for juvenile delinquents. Time in that school taught me anger, resentment, and bigotry. I endured negativity of so many kinds. You never wanted to make eye contact when walking and kept your head down. The fights were never one to one. "Let's kick her ass" or "your ass is grass" would be the call for a group to fight an individual. It was horrible. I remember my friend telling me that her older sister and brother's friends came home from Vietnam. They were white and were stabbed on Francis Lewis Blvd. The guy's abdomen was slashed and his intestines exposed. A friend trained in the service held them inside his gut until the police came.. I learned they eventually died from Agent Orange. So sad to make it home from the war and get stabbed by your fellow countrymen. Nightmares showed me pictures of my family being killed. My mom raising six children was mugged while walking home from work. The guys stole her pocket book and she lost everything, including the envelope with her paycheck. What a life! I was forever on high alert, always in panic mode.

Summer ended and I went to my new school, Linden Junior High 192. "Oh my god! I thought the elementary was bad. This was a free for all!" I felt something hit me really hard in the head as I was changing classes one day. I turned to see six blacks girls standing in a line looking at me with their hands behind their backs as if to say," you want to know who hit it you? You will be jumped if you defend yourself." I saw a dead stare in all of them. It amazed me how they all stood like soldiers. It was a planned affront. Who does this in a civilized world? I hurried to my next class. Why bother going to school, I learned nothing! I took up space. I wanted to learn but it was impossible for *any* of us.

A police guard accompanied us to the bathroom, letting us in one at a time. I guess it was better than having try to remove your clothes. Imagine all the money spent on this inferior educational institution! This was the sixties. You talk about bullying? These experiences define bullying: physical, verbal, and social abuse. I have seen it all. One day in typing class - they called it typing but it was just to pass time – a new student arrived. She was a very pretty white girl carrying a schedule in her hand. I was so happy to have someone like me. I wasn't the only reject! She had beautiful blue eyes and gorgeous red flowing hair. I always kept mine tied back. They were so jealous of her calling, her names while the teacher watched. I told her not to listen to them and that she was very pretty

33

They were not walking on desks in this class because the typewriters were on the desks, instead they would throw the desk over. One girl threw a spitball, hitting the pretty new girl in the eye. This was great entertainment for them and they laughed hysterically. They hated our hair. She found out which girl did it and beat her ass. I knew the fight was on. Desks were turned over. How dare she defend herself! The teacher ran out to protect herself! We were hostages and some gathered in front of the door so no one could leave. The police came and no one was arrested.

So many victims of this racial injustice have died or moved on with their lives. I want the world to know that I carried this anguish too long. The black students would say that white people have everything. Junior high was like I attended prison every day. Fights began without reason. I hated school and cut classes as much as possible. Who would have thought school in our country would be a place where you could lose your life at any time? Violence was everywhere.

The hate overflowed. One day in home room a kid began banging her fist on the desk, saying, "we shall overcome!" Soon the whole class of black kids would be doing the same. The teacher said nothing. I was so happy when the bell rang only to experience something else. The lunchroom was a disaster. Using regular plates before getting smart and changing to plastic, these became frisbees. Broken plates were everywhere. I stopped going and I tried so very hard to avoid confrontation. There was no escape. One day a girl said I called her a name so that someone would beat me up. She lied saying I was making fun of her family. Fear and anxiety followed me. The dismissal bell at the 3pm was the worst. Although I only had to get four blocks to my home, it was like running a gauntlet.. There were no constraints. You were not safe anywhere in that area in Queens.

One night I heard lots of noise downstairs only to find a man was trying to get into the house my brother and sister kept trying to push him out the door. He finally left. The hate was so widespread in this town. I did not see any happiness anywhere. My childhood was ruined. I started stuttering when I spoke. My dad didn't understand why this was happening. He guided me to think of the word first and to speak slowly. This helped and I no longer stutter.

The neighborhood was a living presence that controlled everyone. What to wear... where to look.. what I could and couldn't say. Everything was an issue. One was forced to conform to others' overt jealousy and hatred. I wanted to be myself and I wanted to know my natural coloring was not a bad thing. Any second a riot could erupt. You didn't know if your home would be there when you came home. It was like some terrible futuristic world where survival was all that remained of society. Some whites became turn coats to avoid being attacked. This culture was one of enjoying the minority of whites fight each other. There seemed no way out of this mad house. Violence, bigotry, and jealousy fueled it.

People say that racism is more widespread today. I disagree, it was always there. The internet has brought awareness. I have cried and carried the scars with me. I have felt so wounded and I hid my past filled with pain. I would wonder if I could be sitting next to people on trains and busses if they were among the perpetrators of my horrible past. Who killed the girl just taking a bus. I am grateful for those who watched over me and tried to help me. I have learned that many survivors of this area and time are still afraid and unwilling to share their tales. Some of the victims have turned into hard-core drug addicts to cope. As a child I knew little about coping mechanisms. Some would hear my story and wonder why my parents failed to move. Money or the lack of it kept them stuck. The house held the investment of all their savings.

I moved to Brooklyn to live with my grandma, aunt, and cousins. This neighborhood was not any better. However, I did attend Sacred Heart Catholic school in the 8 th grade. It wasn't as bad as 192. When neighborhoods became intolerable, parents sent their kids to catholic school. As one race started to dominate the schools, white kids could turn on each other. At first I stuck out like a sore thumb but was finally accepted. There was a girl in my class who hung around with blacks and

Spanish because she was afraid of them. I was trying to avoid any violence or confrontation because I lived with my grandma and she didn't need problems. My grandma was a good woman and no bother to anyone. She was friends with most of the people in her parish. I was not about to be disrespectful to her.

Being skinny I became the girl's target. She would call me Ginny and hit me. I would take her abuse every day. She used me as a target to make others laugh and think she was rough and tough because I did not want to respond for fear that my grandmother would get sick or hurt by me fighting or having issues in school. I was trying very hard to learn. I have very curly hair and she would make fun of that. Returning to school I would watch her with her group of friends under the Brooklyn Queens Expressway, smoking. They'd say,"there she is; you can't tell the front from the back. She is so skinny her legs are like toothpicks." I used to feel so ugly and awkward. I knew as soon as I saw her she would belittle me. Everyone would laugh. I ran from one situation only to find another. I guess learning was not an option for me. I could not concentrate. I did not tell my grandma or anyone because I did not want to upset them. I did not want any of my relatives to think it was me who was initiating this type of behavior.

Violence surrounded me everyday in Queens and I only wanted an education. Now it followed me to Brooklyn. The bully hit me in the head with a geography book one day while I walked under the 21 expressway. The pain hit me and I saw her laughing hysterically as she and her friends watched. She contemptuously called me **Dago, Ginny**, or **wop**. I never made fun of her dirty catholic school uniform or anyone else. I knew what it was like to be a target of ridicule. I was in so much pain and humiliation that my grandma heard me crying. I told grandma that I was an object of ridicule. This girl felt free to kick me and make fun of me because I was quiet and she knew I would not hit back. I didn't want problems for my grandmother. I told her she said we were stupid Ginnies. My grandma said she would talk to the nuns and get this strengthen out. I begged her not to do so because only more blacks and the Spanish would gang up on me. She threatened to get her friends from Sands Junior High to hurt me. Grandma did talk to the nuns and the victimization grew worse. But this girl didn't know that I could defend myself. One day she kicked me brutally in the knee and my grandma said, "you gonna kicka her ass now!" I was shocked!

The day she was absent I asked one of the black girls if she planned to jump into the fight if I went against this girl. Her response was that this girl deserved it for the way she treated me. I said OK. We talked and I happened to know her cousin in Queens who told her this white girl could fight. She asked me why I never fought her earlier. I told her that I loved my grandma, she was paying for my school, and I didn't want her to have any problems. Now I knew it was show time. I wanted to get her where everyone would see her go down. I knew I was not going down.

This skinny bone was built for speed. She was on the chunky side. That made her feel as if I was an easy take down for her. She felt powerful with all her ridicule and taunting. When you ignore someone acting this way, the bad escalates. They feel powerful.

I do not think there was one part of my body she had not made fun of. I remembered the day well. It was a Thursday and her pal was always absent on Thursday. This was my Thursday. The teacher told the girl to give the class handouts and left. When she came to my desk she said," what you looking at?" I said,"I am looking you." I could see the shock in her eyes. She proceeded to say,"I will punch you in the mouth here with the teacher in the hallway." I snickered; I knew I had a good right punch. I got up and said," here is my mouth, punch it." She was still surprised that I was standing my ground. I let her think about it for a moment and then punched her in the mouth. She was knocked silly. I sent her right into the side blackboard. Then her head swung backwards. I gave her another shot in the side of her face. She was a very easy target. She had no experience with fighting. She didn't know what hit her. That was my famous right-handed Buttafuoco punch. Next I grabbed that long ponytail that looked like a real horse tail and put her head on the desk, pounding the side of her face. I kept one hand tightly on the ponytail. I purposely did this to have her in a locked position. It was only a 3-step process. I told her to tell the class what I was. "Am I Italian or a Ginnie? "" What are Italians, are they stupid?""Tell the class that you are sorry for making fun of me and calling me stupid."She did. She was crying at the same time. I was ahead of my time. Now women box all the time.

When the nun returned, I made the girl tell her that she had begun it all. I still went to Mother Superior's office and was hit with a paddle but I only felt a great sense of relief. My self-worth and power were back! I could walk wherever I want in the school and not worry about being the brunt of jokes. She looked disheveled and like a shattered pig. Me? I had nothing but a couple of creases in my blouse and it needed to be tucked back into my skirt. The news traveled fast. All my cousins heard about my fight. My grandmother was so happy too. I turned the tables on my tormentor. The ones she thought were her friends slapped me five. They realized that I knew how to fight-not with my mouth but with my hands. When pursuing another white kid to pick on to preserve herself, she picked the wrong one. She never bothered me again.

To save face she began tormenting a pretty new girl from Italy with an accent. I helped her with English. I would help translate words for her. I was a bit confused because my tormentor's Spanish friends had an accent but she never picked on them. This girl called the new student an Italian word meaning whore. My new friend was appalled. I told the aggressor to stop and leave her alone. She wouldn't. I said, "did you forget what happened to you?" Rage filled me, "Do you want another beating? LEAVE HER ALONE!" She was scared! I would never again allow her to abuse anyone else in class. I hate violence and its aftermath but I do believe you must defend and respect yourself. If you don't, others will not respect you.

My poor older brother had his share of racism. He, too, had knives pulled on him. My brother was a light Italian with rosy cheeks and the kids would make fun of him, calling him, whitey and Rosy. I went to White Castle for hamburgers, keeping an eye on my bike. We had one to share for all our siblings. I ran out when I saw a black boy on my bike. I told him to get off but he refused. He called to his friends across the street and they threatened me, saying they would kill me. One guy came over and pulled a zip gun on me, demanding I let the boy have the bike. No one helped. I was able to push him off the bike, jumped on, and they chased me. I dropped my hamburgers and they caught me. They pushed me off the bike and I hit the pavement. They made such a spectacle that they ran. Cars were beeping. There was no one to help me. I finally got home; I was safe and I still had my bike. You never knew what your day was going to be.

Halloween was another free for all. While happily going trick-or-treating and collecting as much candy as possible, the kids would call each other to steal the white kid's candy. Halloween was always a mischievous time. I felt so bad after collecting candy only to have it taken from me. For Halloween in Brooklyn, I dressed like a boy who was a bum. A guy stuck a knife to my throat to steal my candy. My two cousins ran. I did not want to release my bag. I made up a story and said, "you'll be very sorry if you cut me." He heard the strength in my voice and the guy could feel it. They really thought I was a guy and took off running. I got all of our bags back. My aunt came out and called me a brave girl. I was developing a persona which had no fear. I was becoming insensitive to danger.

I was home from school one day and heard the doorbell ring. Grandma told me to answer the door. She asked me in Italian who was at the door. I told her it was a colored woman who wanted to know if we had an apartment to rent. Grandma said no that this was her building and that her daughter and grandkids lived upstairs. The woman started screaming, "you are lying, you just don't want coloreds in your building." My grandma told her to leave. The woman said she would report my grandma to the NAACP. Grandma said," I no care, this is my house." Grandma asked me," what is a naap?" I said I do not really know but I knew it was not good. I was learning all kinds of negative things as a child.

I would go home to visit my brothers and sisters in Queens on the weekend and leave Sunday night to go back to Brooklyn. I was still having a hard time in school because I missed all those years. I was trying so hard but it was as if there was a block in my mind. Grandma kept insisting that I not go. I needed to take the L train to Jamaica. Grandma told me they were killing people on the trains coming home from work. People were beaten and stabbed. Fires were started. My grandma did not want me to take the train. That was the day after Martin Luther King was assassinated on April 4, 1968 in Memphis. I traveled alone..

There were riots all over the U.S . My friend's brother was getting off a bus and a woman accused him of raping her daughter. She lied about this little 8 year-old boy so he would be beaten coming off the bus. This recording has played in my mind for years. I cannot imagine not releasing it. This occurrence 23 of racial injustice is not new. I lived it. My body shows the effects of my childhood beatings. Because of the years abuse I developed a learning disability. The trauma created.

I told my friend, the man with the stroke, that I was writing a book about our lives then. He seemed to smile. He was the one who was bite by the dog and accused of rape. My friend his sister, told me she saw her father being jumped by bunch black men in front of her house. How terrifying that was. He was just coming home from work. My dad had a similar experience. My dad was coming home from work he was attacked from behind with large, thick glass 7 Up bottles. They would never have won from the front – he was a great fighter/boxer. My friend moved to Brooklyn, too. There was no one to help us and I really believed we would never reach adulthood.

I did make it. It was rough and I quit high school. I thought I was unintelligent. The word dumb would repeat in my head. I had no needed skills for the workforce. I tried several times to get my GED in Boces. I tried night school only to drop out. I couldn't keep up with the work. The large GED book was very intimidating. I had no basic knowledge or foundation to build on. I lost the most crucial years. I failed to find a way to learn everything I lost in those few years. Others I knew had the same difficulties. What was wrong with me? Something stunted my growth and ability to learn. I would watch people graduate and wonder how they did it.

I had to work in menial jobs because I had no skills. I felt I had no future.

Some had died at the hands of our attackers and others suffered while trying to survive. College seemed totally out of reach. I had so much fear even to try. I knew I did not have the basic knowledge to pass high school. I was embarrassed to tell anyone. We moved to a new neighborhood and I started 9th grade there. I could not keep up with the work at all. I always carried insecurities, always on guard for a fight.

This neighborhood was so nice. The kids went to school to learn. I was the only one who seemed to have a bad attitude. I talked to my friend who I grew up in Queens. I wanted her to come here. It was so nice and quiet. you could walk freely. We talked her mom into her coming to my school my mother was going to let her use our address. She started school with us; we were so happy. One day she left and her family moved to Deer Park, Long Island. We did not see each other much anymore but we always had the connection of our past. I would see her after long periods of time and we would submerge those terrifying memories in our minds and hearts. I had issues where I could not sit for too long. I would be disruptive as a distraction so no one would think me stupid. I didn't want the teacher to call on me. I didn't want the other kids to know that I was stupid. When we had tests, I would panic all I could see was an empty paper. Sometimes I would not turn them in. I could not keep up it was very frustrating. I would go blank with fear. My heart would race, I could not do this. I had poor retention skills. I eventually quit high school.
I felt inside that I was a failure. Others were moving on to college and other institutions. Not me. I was left behind. I had to go through life without an education. I heard my local high school had a program at night. It was called night school to help get your High school diploma so I signed up. You had to buy this gigantic book. I looked through the book with excitement and then thought, "Oh, no. I don't know any of this. I was still lost in this class but happy that the people with me were adults and they wanted to learn. I still couldn't keep up. I again felt like a failure and quit. I was so saddened. I looked for job after job. Eventually I enrolled in the Boces Adult education in Hempstead. I was taking my GED and key

punch classes. Just as in Queens, no one was listening in class and fights were breaking out. I felt I was attracting the wrong people. I shouted in my head, "all I want is an education!" I dropped out of that 24 class, too. I was weary of fighting and hate. I saw the difference in the Elmont and NYC schools. If only I had that opportunity to learn. I was 16 years-old and a drop out.

I felt inadequate most of my life when it came to education. I cried so many times with this emptiness in my heart. I knew it would affect my life. This was another hole in my heart along with the trauma of my younger years. I tried to get my GED a few times only to fail. I couldn't understand what was wrong.
The only thing I really had going for me was my art. I was very good in it but I did not want anything to do with art. Where can a child go? Who do you talk to? I felt I would be thought simply defiant and labeled as one who didn't want an education. I tried to go on with my life. School was nothing but, a
scary time in my life. I did not know if I would come home or not. Parents were afraid for their children, too. I thought of all the kids who died and the ones alive who were going through the same thing as I was.

My friend and her brother had many issues in school as well. We all had a horrible education. We all just took up space. I hated sitting there all day. The days seemed so long. We all felt inferior when it came to education. That was something inaccessible to us. It's so important for a child to have a starting
point or a baseline in education to be able to move to the next level. Ours was destroyed and this took its toll on us. Always surrounded by violence, a child lives in fight or flight mode. My days were consumed by fear without thought or reason. I knew in my heart that it had a bearing on me achieving
my goals but had no idea how to correct and fix this. Who understands only the ones that suffered? I wanted desperately to learn. I knew it was so important. I could not catch that star. I knew my dreams were shattered. Where do you go to start school at 16 to get a 5th grade education? I

needed all these years from 5th grade. How does a 16-year-old go back to 5 th grade? It was so embarrassing. Therefore, I went on with my life. I never would tell anyone I did not have a High School diploma. I wanted to reach for different jobs but had no high school diploma and was disqualified. I finally got a job at McDonald's. I was glad I did not have to do the register because I would have to count change.

I was the drink girl. All I did was make drinks. I was petrified to do the register, I knew I couldn't. One day, they put me on the register; I was shorting change constantly and they returned to the drinks station. I was so glad I was receiving a paycheck without having to do anything that required math. I was only working part time and I needed another job so I got a job at a men's clothing store. They were training me on the register. I was so scared. I could not count change back for big bills or small ones. So, they made me a floor sales girl. I worked McDonald's in the day and the men's clothing store at night. This was perfect for me. I knew in my heart this was the only type of job I could do I could not handle money at all.

I knew college was unattainable. These jobs were all right but I knew I wanted more from life. At least I had work. Years later I got a job in a diner as a hostess. I had to handle money and I was so scared. I knew I could not do it. I worked the breakfast shift. My addition and subtraction were the worst and
that's what I had to know. The customers would bring the bills up to me and I had to make change. I was so afraid of making mistakes but that seemed the only outcome. Breakfast was easy because the menu didn't change. Most of the breakfast specials were $3.50. I memorized 1 dollar and fifty cents if
they gave me a 5.00-dollar bill. I started memorizing the change back. I knew what to give back from a 5-dollar. Also, if they gave me a hundred I would break the hundred to a smaller bill. I was lost otherwise. I learned all from memorization. I thought that was pathetic, dysfunctional, and incompetent.

I knew that I was limited in my capabilities as an adult. How could I begin

at 4th grade level? It was so upsetting. I carried two secrets into this fast-paced world: my childhood trauma of violence and racism and my lack of education.. My early school years were damaged and now I found l had a new problem -
lack of survival skills for employment. Where do you go for a job? I was fired as a waitress. It would have been good to have had calculators then. It was very hard for me to learn anything new. It was as if I was in slow motion. If I started something new, I had to repeat it many times. I was street smart but that wouldn't pay the bills. I started housecleaning. That became so hard and backbreaking. I started a job in a school district cleaning and that grew laborious but paid more than minimum wage. I eventually quit that job, too.

I went next to a job in sales away from registers and need for calculations. I stayed in that job for many years. It was the only way to pay my bills. I became an independent contractor. I started using my art skills and became a makeup artist. I took some classes and received a certification as a makeup artist.
You did not need a diploma for this – I felt safe. I always stayed in the safe zone and learned what required a diploma and what did not. I worked all over NYC in the late 80's and 90's. I also worked weddings - brides and bridesmaids models for photo shoots. I loved it but still wanted an education. I always tried to read and stay up to date on current events but in my heart I was hurting. I continued to work, doing the best that I could. Another secret to carry. I saw people in Manhattan and thought they must work in nice offices. I knew that would never be me. Still, I wondered what it would be like to work in an office there.

My dream was to live in Manhattan. I continued doing makeup for years and working as a sales person. I was a very good at sales. I just went on with my life. I moved into selling fragrances which was much easier. I still did not need to handle money. I realized I repeated recordings of my mind about past trauma with all the hatred. I knew it was passed from generation to generation. I was the one who suffered. I can pull the intense feelings of that emotion watching media stories. My heart starts to race and my fist clinch. I go in survival mode. As I am writing and editing, my heart races and the tears flow. I am here to give voice to our experiences. We don't share this in the media today.

Some say you cannot live in the past. How can one let go when it upset my whole life? I missed years of education. I was brutalized. I saw terrors. My mind returns to those who died when I listen to stories of racism. My friends were killed because they were white. When I see a video of blacks saying they
were signaled out because of racism. My mind tells me I want to see the whole video not just one side. Because I was torn between right and wrong, I was a wounded warrior. I survived and others did not. More than a small piece of me died inside. Whenever I see an act of hate, my mind goes back to my
past. I also see dissonance when we equate racial hatred only with one race. I hope my book will bring some healing from having the story of our perspective told. I feel how slanted internet comments can be. Our lives as whites were hell.

There were times when working that I was accused of racism. I remember working in retail and a black women came in to buy a lipstick which was out of stock. I suggested Revlon and she shouted at me,"why are you suggesting Revlon because I am black and you think I have no money in my pocket?" I see both sides of this horrible encounter with racism. The symbol of racism shouldn't be a tool. I see both ends of the tool. I have never shared much of my story. Sometimes we try to stand our ground. The world around is moving you must move with it. You must stay strong.

Each one of us has become different with our experiences. I want to tell everyone that change is possible. A good life is like a plant. It needs the right nutrients and lots of sunlight. By shining my own flashlight on my past, I am looking clearly at truth. It is my truth and I am made stronger by viewing
many sides.

VOICES NEVER HEARD!!

When we can accept that we have experienced trauma, we are connected to the world. It's not pretty. It is real.

Epilogue

I went on with my life and I eventually started to get an education at 52-years old. My son was attending school at Nassau Community College when he heard of an exciting program. Getting 24 college credits would allow you to receive a high school diploma. My son is to thank for this. My dream could materialize. I had returned to Boces Adult Education. I was tested and told I had a fourth grade education. Although I cried I was validated. I lacked an education not that I was unteachable.

I began to fix this at the local college and applied for the 24-credit program. I graduated in 2017, with a Bachelor of Science degree. I also had a radio program called *Victims Speak Out*. Now the voices from my past are alive and being heard. I am also writing a book. I want the world to know that you can rise above horrific circumstances. I am not the dummy I thought I was. I have street smarts and book smarts. Most of all my heart calls me to help others who are suffering.

I went from 4th grade to a bachelor's degree. I made it!! Every day I studied for hours. I worked at the school as a bus attendant so I could utilize the time to go to school at night. I really enjoyed college. It was the best experience I ever had. I was embarrassed at first to be in my fifties going to school. Never
think that you cannot succeed. Just keep going! Everything moves and we need to move with it. There is an Italian saying, "stagnant water stinks." I want to be fresh water and fresh water to others. I want to be a light to others who feel they can't move forward. The box does have a cover and it can be opened
and closed. You must keep it open.

Life is wonderful! You need to absorb what you can and share it with others. This will release them from their private box. No matter how hard the path seems, take the steps toward your goals. My education was the biggest achievement to me.

VOICES NEVER HEARD!!

I had a talk show that gave me a sense of happiness to have people open up and talk about what's hurting them inside. I am also an actor. I was on the *Soprano's*. You have to follow your heart's desire. Most of all be an example to others in a positive way. I spoke out and feel so good about it. Not all may
find justice satisfied but our lives and experiences have mattered. Those who have died I am your voice!!
Your voices have been heard!!! I dedicate this book to you!

My husband wanted me to add something to my book. He wants the world to know that as many times as he heard my stories and trials I suffered, my story never changed. What he is trying to say is that I am not a liar and a true victim of Racism.

Work Cited

https://www.ncab.org.au/bullying-advice/bullying-for-parents/types-of-bullying

https://theblackdetour.com/5-race-riots-of-the-1960s-in-america/

https://www.blackpast.org/aaw/vignette_aahw/rodney-king-riot-1992/

https://www.encyclopedia.com%3E.http//scholar.library.miami.edu/sixties/urba nRi   ots.php

https://kinginstitute.stanford.edu/encyclopedia/assassination-martin-luther-king-j r

https://www.politico.com/magazine/story/2015/08/school-busing-civil-rights-12 1077

"Race Riots of the 1960s." U*X*L Encyclopedia of U.S. History. . Encyclopedia.com. 26 Feb. 2019

https://www.politico.com/magazine/story/2015/08/school-busing-civil-rights-12 1077

https://en.wikipedia.org/wiki/Tawana_Brawley_rape_allegations

http://scholar.library.miami.edu/sixties/urbanRiots.php

https://www.blackpast.org/aaw/vignette_aahw/rodney-king-riot-1992/

https://www.ncab.org.au/bullying-advice/bullying-for-parents/types-of-bullying/

https://theblackdetour.com/5-race-riots-of-the-1960s-in-america/

https://en.wikipedia.org/wiki/Tawana_Brawley_rape_allegations

VOICES NEVER HEARD!!

ABOUT THE AUTHOR

Marylyn Buttafuoco Aguilar is a New York native, born May 6, 1955. Living through the turbulence of the Civil Rights movement of the 1960's, she found herself at the receiving end of terrifying bigotry as one of a very few caucasians in the ghetto-like atmosphere. Marylyn is a strong Italian American who lives as a survivor of such upheaval. Her greatest wish today stands as making a difference for others who have stories to tell.

VOICES NEVER HEARD!!

VOICES NEVER HEARD!!

www.ingramcontent.com/pod-product-compliance
Lightning Source LLC
Chambersburg PA
CBHW050339290526
45785CB00006B/2560